To:

From:

Date:

My
Dance With God

Author & Illustrator
Kathleen L. Rousar

K.L
ROUSAR

My Dance with God
by Kathleen L. Rousar

First published in 2013 by **Velatura Press LLC**
www.klrousar.com

Unless otherwise stated, all Biblical references are adapted from Young's Literal Translation

ISBN-13: 978-0-9800454-6-8
ISBN-10: 0-9800454-6-0
First Printing, 2013
Printed in the United States of America

Library of Congress Cataloging-in-Publication Data
Rousar, Kathleen L.
  My Dance with God / by Kathleen L. Rousar.
  ISBN-13: 978-0-9800454-6-8
  REL012020   Religion : Christian Life - Devotional
  REL077000   Religion : Faith

Library of Congress Control Number: 2013934464

Velatura Press™ Minneapolis, Minnesota USA

Dedication

-For Sarah Marie-
Your courage has been a
constant inspiration to me.
You are a beautiful
daughter of our Father.

Introduction

Have you ever been desperate for comfort or felt unable to comfort another in need? *My Dance with God* was born out of just such a need in my life. I hope that this book will serve as a gift to yourself, or as one you will give to others, to provide a visual place of rest for your eyes and heart through scripture and the images of my artwork.

Through many trials I have longed for a simple Biblical-based resting place of hope and encouragement. As I sketched and painted I sought comfort from God's Word. The Bible verses in this book are the verses that God brought to my heart as I worked on the artwork.

My Dance With God can be read as a devotional, from front to back, or by jumping around. In either case, grab your favorite cup of tea and sit back and relax. I hope that sharing my journey will bring you hope and inspire you to allow God to reveal His compassion for you.

After this introduction, I begin the book with a copy of a page taken from one of my daily journals, which I call, "*My Letters to God.*" The page represents the beginning of my journey with God over the last few years, from hopelessness to hope. I was hopeless, until I learned that our hope comes through the promises in God's Word, no matter what our feelings or circumstances may be.

One of my challenges was a complicated health issue that, for a time, often prevented me from using my dominant right hand. I began writing the journals as a means to teach myself to use my left hand when I was unable to use my right. Recently I have learned that artists throughout the ages would discipline themselves to draw and paint with their non-dominant hand. They felt that using their non-dominant hand would tap into the other side of the brain, therefore enhancing their creativity. After years of practice I now use both hands to draw, paint and write.

About the sketches . . .

I do not know much about ballet and I had never drawn or painted a ballerina before. I just felt compelled to begin to draw and eventually to paint them. I used my own photographed images of dancers for reference material. The images in the first section of this book are my rough pencil sketches of a young dancer in training. I was not going to include these crude sketches; after all, they are not my "best" work. However, something Beatrix Potter wrote got me thinking: "*I cannot rest, I must draw, however poor the result, and when I have a bad time come over me it is a stronger desire than ever.*"

Being predominantly self-taught, I have felt weak and tempted to give up many times. But I thought of Paul, when he wrote in 2 Corinthians 12:9: God said, "*My grace is sufficient for you, for my power is made perfect in weakness.*" Then Paul said, "*Therefore I will boast all the more gladly about my weaknesses, so that Christ's power may rest on me.*"

When I am weak and seek my strength from God, I experience that very "strong desire" of which Beatrix spoke. I took this as a challenge to view the rough sketches as a reason to strive for a more refined skill. In this way God was using my own weakness to inspire me. So I share with you these weak sketches, along with the strong promises in God's Word.

As I finished each sketch I would study the Bible and pray. I would ask God to speak to my heart and to bring to mind a special verse for each one of the sketches. Through His leading, I was encouraged to keep my focus on Him. These verses gave me courage, and that just as Paul said, when I am weak God is strong. I can trust Him as I practice God's promises in His Word.

I tried to capture a sense of the dancer's focus as I sketched. As you focus on each related verse, try to take the position of the dancer and allow your body to worship God. I hope that when you view the sketches and read the verses you can learn to focus on God and rely on the power of Christ to make you strong.

In the next section, titled, "*God loves you this way*," I include an invitation to accept Christ. If you have not already accepted Him as your Lord and Savior, I strongly encourage you to do that now. If you have already taken this step in your life, then please take a moment when you get to this part of the book to pray for anyone that you may know who needs to make Jesus the Lord of their life.

The watercolor paintings comprise the final section. They are images, first of little girls, and then young ladies, practicing – all dressed in traditional ballet costumes. As I was photographing my reference material for these paintings, I was drawn to the fragile beauty of the costume. I was in awe of the contrast between the delicate toile fabric of the tutu and the shiny pink silk slippers, and the harsh reality of the grueling hours of practice it takes to learn to dance.

Initially I began painting the ballerinas in black and white to economize on paint, but with the first one I sensed that I should continue with this simple color scheme. I also understood that the slippers and bow sashes needed to be pink. As I created more paintings, while praying and studying God's Word, I began to see the reasons for the lack of color in the figures, as well as for the pink slippers. When you dance with God He moves your life from simple black and white to full living color. So I carried on painting the slippers and the sash bows in the delicate pink color.

Through these drawings, paintings and Bible verses I hope you see that God is the source of all true love. He wants you to experience that love and take refuge in Him as a daughter of the King. "*God loves you this way.*"

In conclusion I give you these verses, James 1:22-25, from the New Living Translation:
"*Don't just listen to God's Word. You must do what it says. Otherwise, you are only fooling yourselves. For if you listen to the Word and don't obey, it is like glancing at your face in a mirror. You see yourself, walk away, and forget what you look like. But if you look carefully into the perfect law that sets you free, and if you do what it says and don't forget what you heard, then God will bless you for doing it.*"

I pray that the mirror of God's Word helps you look at yourself. As you allow God to show you His love, you can decide if you need to make any changes in your life. My prayer for myself, and for you, is that viewing these paintings and then reading God's Word will increase our capacity to receive God's love. We will then know all the more who we are in Christ as daughters of the King, in order to be better able to give that love away to others.

Dear Father God,

Today i feel fragile i am flawed and cracked like an old leaky pot of clay.

My past has caused this damage. You created me,

You are the potter, i am the clay. Teach me my value in You as You see me as Your daughter in Christ.

— amen —

Love, Kathleen

"The more you reaffirm who you are in Christ, the more your behavior will begin to reflect your true identity!"

Dr. Neil Anderson
Victory Over the Darkness

Job 11:18

And you have trusted because there is hope. You have searched and lie down in safety.

James 4:7

Be subject to God;
stand up against the
devil and he will flee
from you.

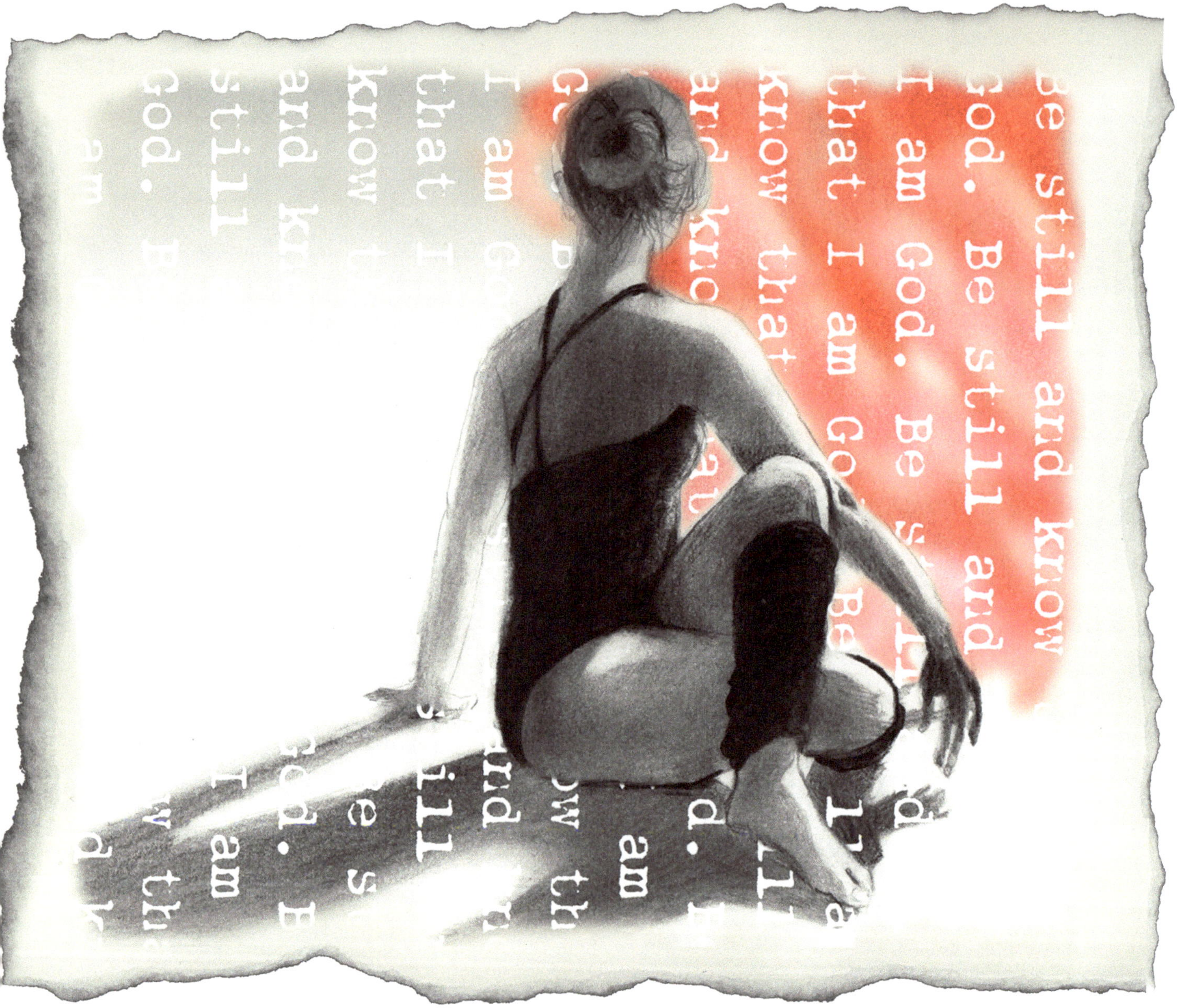
Be still and know
God. Be still and

Psalm 46:10

Be still, and know
that I am God. I am
exalted among the
nations, I am exalted
in the earth.

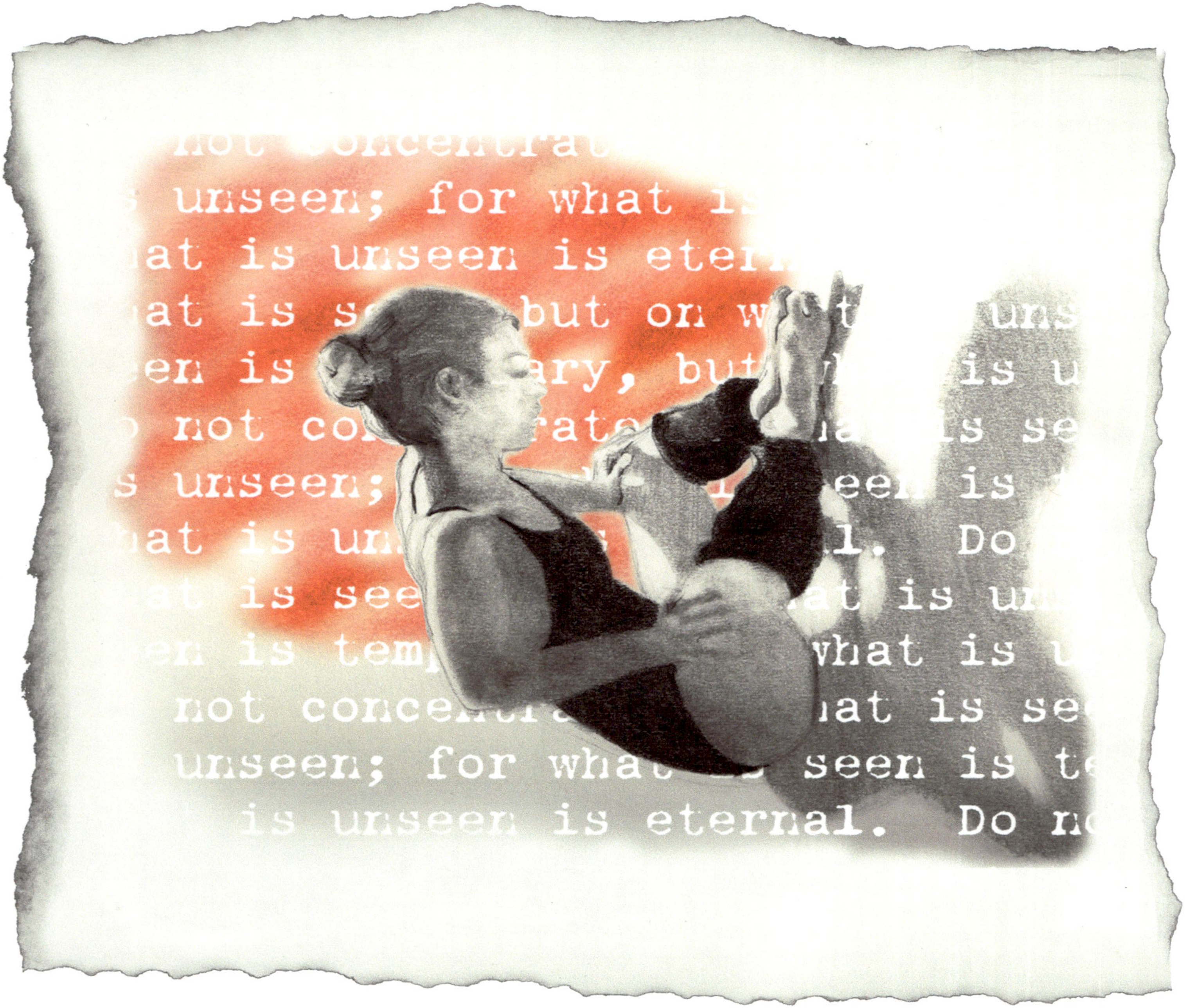

unseen; for what is seen is te
is unseen is eternal. Do no

2 Corinthians 4:18

We are not looking to things that are seen, but to the things not seen; for the things seen are temporary, but the things not seen are forever.

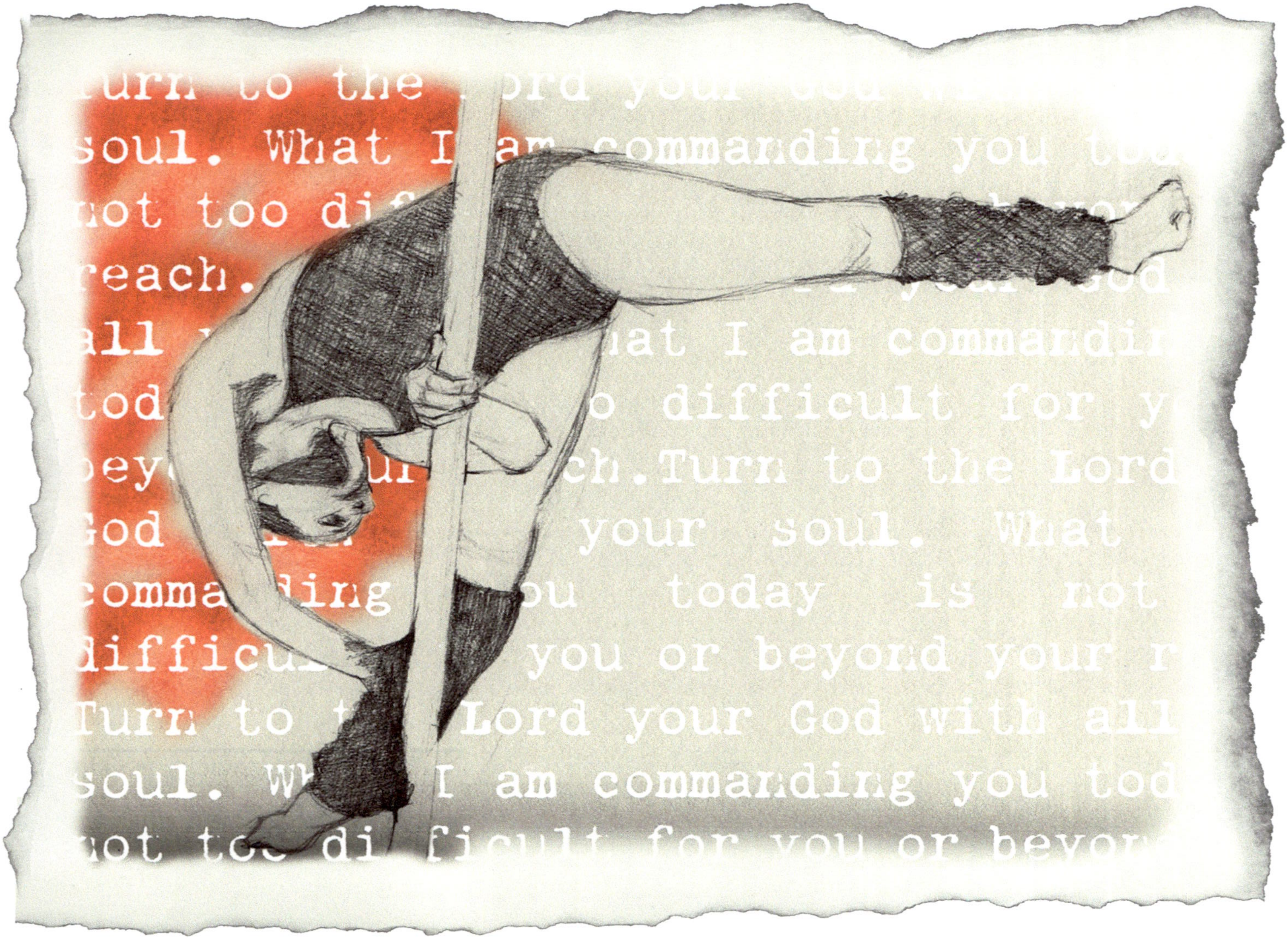

Deuteronomy 30:10 & 11

Turn towards the Lord your God,
with all your heart, and with all your
soul. For this command which I am
commanding you today is not too
wonderful for you, nor is it beyond
your reach.

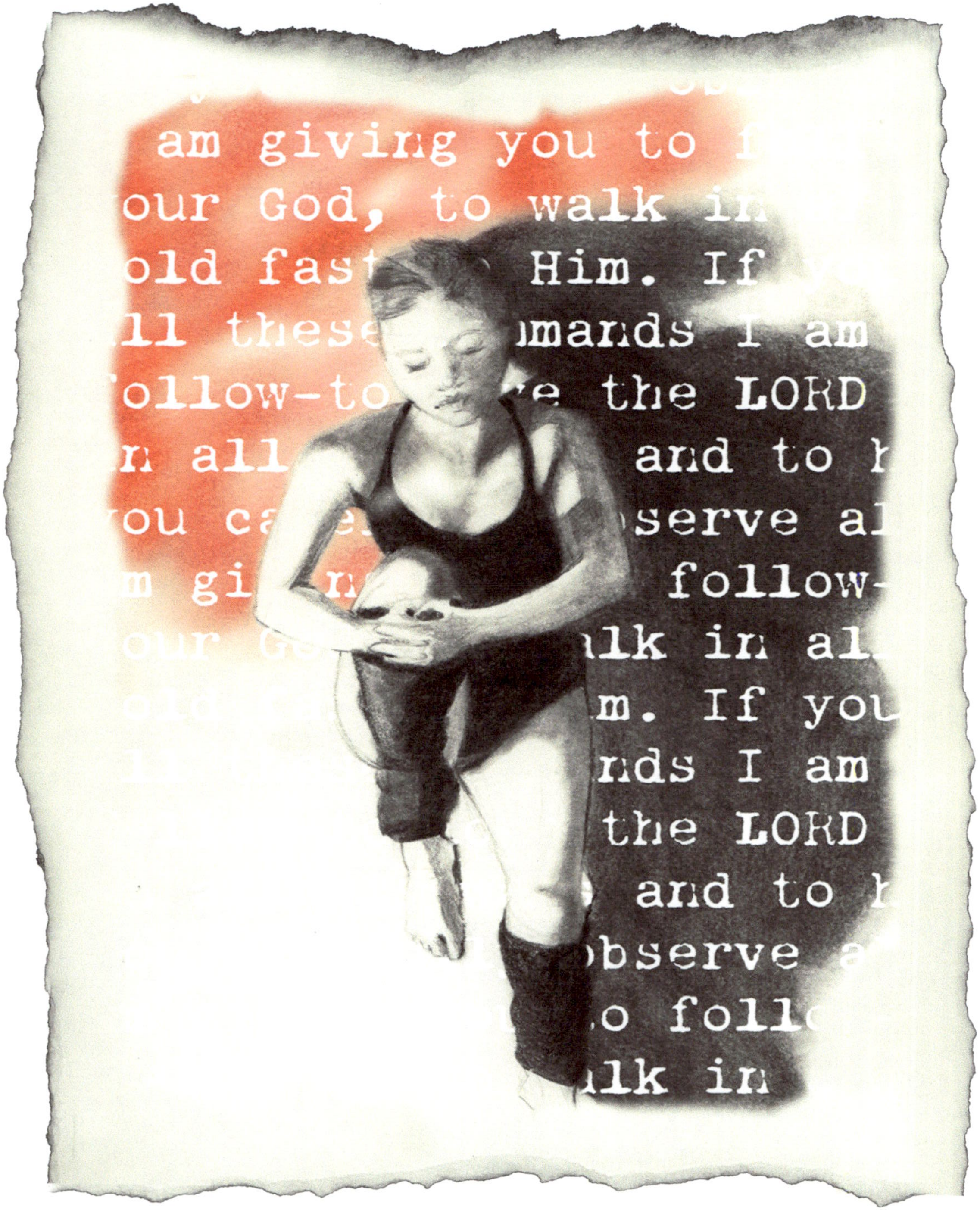

Joshua 23:8

Hold fast to the Lord your God, as you have done to this day.

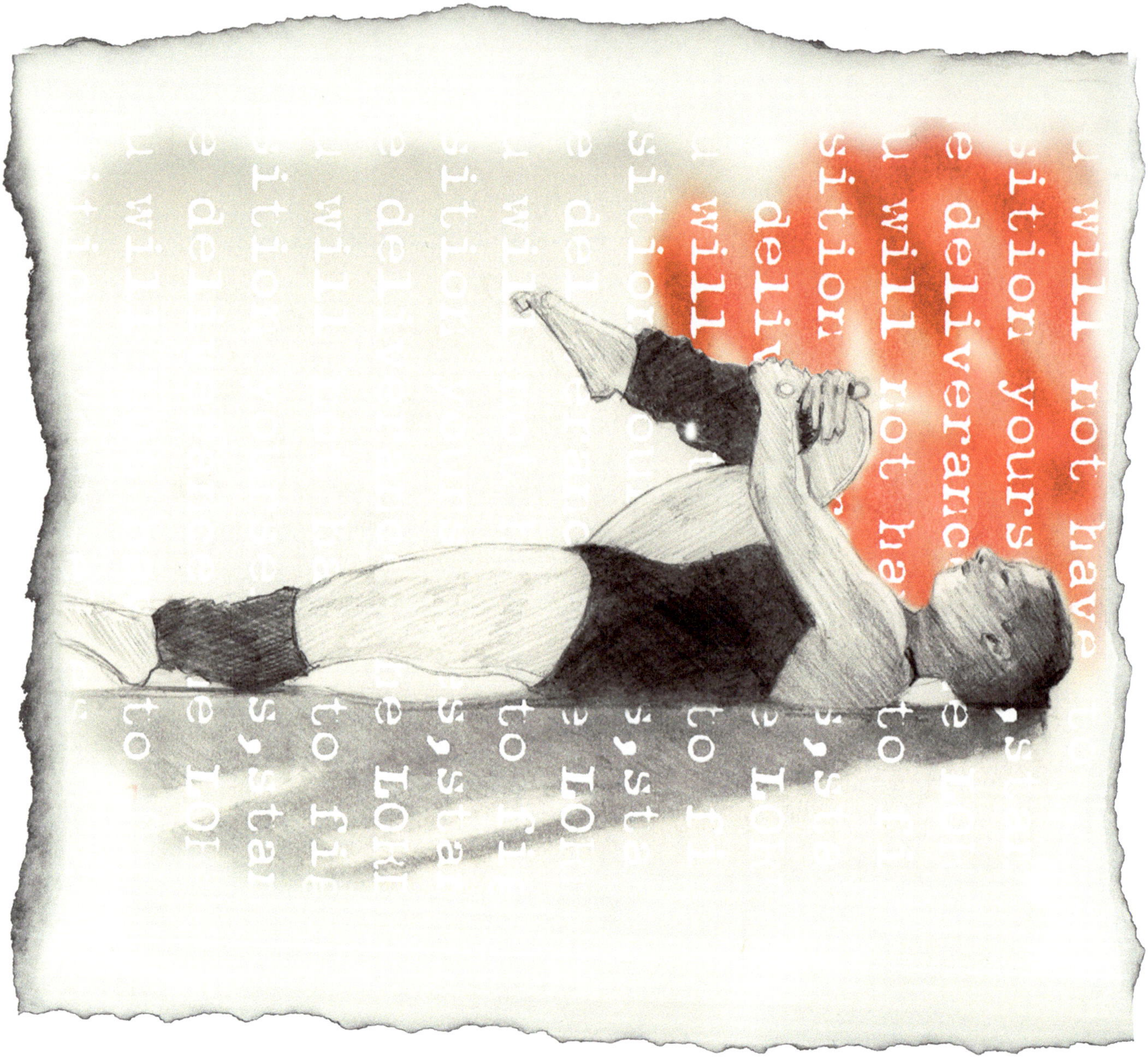

2 Chronicles 20:17

This is not your battle to fight;
stand firm, position yourselves,
and see the deliverance the Lord
will give you.

Psalm 51:10

Create in me a clean
heart, O God, And
renew a right spirit
within me.

Matthew 18:4

Whoever humbles
themselves like a child
is the greatest in the
kingdom of heaven.

RD. Be strong and take heart,
he LORD. Be strong and take heart,
strong and take
strong and ta
Be strong and
in the LORD. Be
all you who hope
all you who
heart, all you who
and all you

Psalm 31:24

Be strong, and He will
strengthen your heart, All
you who wait for God!

God loves you this way . . . .

Do you long to experience God's love?

If so, why not settle this right now? Jesus is the evidence that God has a plan for your life. God loves you so much that He gave you the ultimate gift, His son, to pay the ultimate price by laying down His life for your sin. Even if you were the only human being who ever rebelled against God, He loves you so much that He would have sent Jesus to die just for you.

You may have the thought, "No one else has ever loved me this way" – but God does love you this way, and He wants to personally dwell in your heart.

If you are ready to accept Christ, talk to God now, silently or aloud. Tell him, from your heart that you agree with Him when He said that you need a savior, and that Jesus is that savior. Confess that Jesus is the Son of God and that He died for your sins and rose again from the dead. Ask Him to forgive you for your sin and then accept that forgiveness.

God will then become your loving, heavenly Father and you will become His beloved child.

The Lord will then give you another gift, the Holy Spirit, who will enable you to experience the free gift of God's love for you.

Begin to read the Bible* by starting with the book of John, in order to learn more about who God can be in your life. John writes about the teachings of Jesus, which reveal the truth of who you are in Him. You will learn that it is only by accepting the truth about yourself that you can become truly free. This is why Jesus proclaimed in John 8:32, "You will know the truth, and the truth will make you free."

*One of the easiest ways, and actually the very best way to obtain a Bible is to call a local Bible-based church. Let them know that you are a new Christian and that you would like to connect and to learn more about following Christ as your personal savior. You could also go to the website called Bible Gateway (www. biblegateway.com), which provides a searchable, online Bible with over 100 versions to choose from.

Psalm 139:13&14

God, You formed me. You formed me in my mother's womb.

I will praise You, because I am wonderfully made. Wonderful are Your works, and my soul knows it is well.

My substance was not hidden from You when I was made in secret. When I was knit together in the depths of the earth, Your eyes saw my unformed body.

1 John 3:1

How Great the love our Father has given to us, that we may be called children of God; because of this the world does not know us, because it did not know Him.

1 Corinthians 13:12

Now we see but a poor reflection in a mirror; then we shall see face to face; now I know in part, and then I shall know fully, even as I am fully known.

Isaiah 40:31

Those who hope in the Lord
will have their strength renewed,
They will rise up as eagles. They
run and are not fatigued. They go
on and do not faint!

Matthew 11:28-30

Come unto Me, all who are laboring and burdened, and I will give you rest. Take up my yoke and learn from Me, because I am meek and humble in heart, and you shall find rest for your souls, for My yoke is easy, and My burden is light.

Psalm 51:10-12

Create in me a clean heart, O God, and renew a right spirit within me. Do not cast me away from Your presence, nor take Your Holy Spirit from me.

Restore to me the joy of Your salvation, and a give me a willing spirit which will sustain me.

Romans 8:28

We know that to those who love
God all things do work together
for good, to those who are called
according to purpose.

Exodus 15:2

The Lord is my strength
and my song, and He is my
salvation: This is my God,
and I glorify Him; God of
my father, and I exalt Him.

Philippians 4:6-7

Be anxious for nothing, but in everything by prayer and supplication, with thanksgiving, let your requests be made known to God; and the peace of God, which surpasses all understanding, shall guard your hearts and your minds in Christ Jesus.

Jeremiah 31:13

Then the young women
shall dance and rejoice, both
young men and old men
together as well. I will turn
their mourning to joy, I will
give them comfort and turn
their sorrow to joy.

Matthew 18:20

'Where there are two or three gathered together, in my name, there am I in the midst of them.'

1 Peter 2:21

For to this you were called,
because Christ also suffered for
you as an example, that you may
follow in his steps.

About me . . .

I have always been creative and intensely interested in expressing myself through painting and drawing. I am in my mid-fifties and am primarily self taught. I began painting full-time a few years ago and I work primarily in watercolor. My reference material comes from life, my imagination and my original photographs. I currently devote my days to painting and intercessory prayer. A few years ago I also began writing and I now keep three daily painting and writing journals. Because I am a Christian I have dedicated my life's work to the glory of God and I want to share the beauty that I see in God's world through my artwork and writing. I am convinced that no matter who you are, how old you are, or what resources you possess, you can discover your own unique, God-given creative ability. I want to share this hope by encouraging you to discover who you are uniquely created to be in Christ. In the future I look forward to getting back to teaching workshops and will continue painting and writing as God leads.

As I share with you a bit of my journey as a Christian, I pray that you will identify with my struggle and find a new hope, as I did, in who God is – your loving Father in Heaven.

I accepted Christ at a young age but even though I have been a Christian for most of my life I have suffered much hardship and I didn't always make the best choices. I never knew my earthly father and the pain of my past left me with a great temptation to blame God for the hurtful actions of others. Through difficult circumstances I lived in the shadows of the wrongs done to me and the guilt over my own mistakes. However, no matter what happened to me in the past the one truth is that God never left me. As long as I sought after Him, He was there. My victory over defeat came when I decided to act on the truth in God's Word, that God is greater than any fear, past or present.

These days as I go into my studio to paint, I don't base my actions on where my work will end up or what people may think. I just go and do my task for the day. I start my day praising God and I no longer wait to feel good to act. Instead, I act and paint and claim that God is with me no matter how my painting time goes. This has changed my focus to praising God and I now thank Him for whatever I am able to do that day. As He said in Isaiah 55:8-9, *"For my thoughts are not your thoughts, neither are your ways my ways," declares the LORD. "As the heavens are higher than the earth, so are my ways higher than your ways and my thoughts than your thoughts."*

When we trust and praise God for who He is, even when we are in the midst of turmoil that we do not understand, our concerns will take on their proper perspective. We can trust that God has a plan, even though we may not see it right now, and know the truth that God is protecting us and working behind the scenes to carry out His perfect plan for our lives.

I once read that before an approaching storm an eagle will seek out a high perch and wait until the first strong winds begin to blow. It then allows those winds to lift it high above the stormy turmoil. I want to encourage you to not give up in whatever storm you may be experiencing right now. You, too, can rise above your past. You can shift your thoughts from the hopelessness of circumstance and place your hope in the Lord. The storms of life do not have to overcome you. You can rise above the storms that bring disappointment, sickness, tragedy and death upon you by allowing the truth of God's power to lift you up, above them like the eagle. God will enable you to ride out the winds of the storm if you trust and place your hope in who He is.

Thank You

-To my husband Darren-
You are the love of my life
and I could have never
done this without your
help and support.

www.ingramcontent.com/pod-product-compliance
Lightning Source LLC
Chambersburg PA
CBHW061356090426
42739CB00003B/45